CHRIS

Do you know everything about your family – your parents, your grandparents, your brothers or sisters, your uncles or aunts? Does your family know everything about you? All families have secrets – they can be big secrets, small secrets, things to laugh about, things to cry about.

Jan lives in Oxford with his English wife Carol, and his father Josef, who is Czech. Jan was born in Prague, but he came to England with his father when he was a baby. He never knew his mother – she died soon after he was born. And he knows nothing about her because his father never talks about her. But Josef still carries a photograph of his wife in his pocket – after all these years.

Carol plays the harp in an orchestra, and the orchestra is giving some concerts in Prague at Christmas. Carol wants to go, and she wants Jan and Josef to go too. 'Prague is a wonderful place,' she says, 'for a family Christmas.'

But there are family secrets waiting for them in Prague – wonderful secrets, happy secrets, and very sad secrets . . .

OXFORD BOOKWORMS LIBRARY
Human Interest

Christmas in Prague

Stage 1 (400 headwords)

Series Editor: Jennifer Bassett
Founder Editor: Tricia Hedge
Activities Editors: Jennifer Bassett and Alison Baxter

For Ralph and Stania Hrdličková

JOYCE HANNAM

Christmas in Prague

OXFORD UNIVERSITY PRESS

OXFORD

UNIVERSITY PRESS

Great Clarendon Street, Oxford OX2 6DP

Oxford University Press is a department of the University of Oxford.
It furthers the University's objective of excellence in research, scholarship,
and education by publishing worldwide in

Oxford New York

Auckland Cape Town Dar es Salaam Hong Kong Karachi
Kuala Lumpur Madrid Melbourne Mexico City Nairobi
New Delhi Shanghai Taipei Toronto

With offices in

Argentina Austria Brazil Chile Czech Republic France Greece
Guatemala Hungary Italy Japan Poland Portugal Singapore
South Korea Switzerland Thailand Turkey Ukraine Vietnam

OXFORD and OXFORD ENGLISH are registered trade marks of
Oxford University Press in the UK and in certain other countries

ISBN-13: 978 0 19 422938 8
ISBN-10: 0 19 422938 6

Printed in Hong Kong

ACKNOWLEDGEMENTS
Illustrated by: Gerry Grace

CONTENTS

1

Christmas 1957

It is night, and the fields near the village are white with snow. The village is quiet, but not everybody is sleeping. Eyes are watching the roads and the fields near the village, because this is Czechoslovakia and the year is 1957. Across the fields, only half a kilometre away, is the Austrian border, but the people of Czechoslovakia are not free to go to Austria. The border guards watch day and night – and they carry guns.

In a house in the village a man and a woman are talking. The woman holds a six-month-old baby boy in her arms.

The border guards watch day and night.

She is excited, but she is afraid, too.

'Tell me again,' she says. 'Did he get to Austria all right last night?'

'Yes, he did,' the man says. 'Nobody saw him, nobody heard him. But last night was easy because the sky was dark. Tonight it's more difficult – look at that moon!'

'But it's Christmas night,' the woman says, 'and the guards are drinking in the guardhouse, yes?'

'That's true,' says the man, 'but sometimes they come out and drive up and down the road for a time. So you must be careful, and you must run fast – very fast.' He looks at his watch. 'It's time to go.'

The woman puts on a white coat and a white hat. The baby wears a white coat too, and the woman carries him on her back.

'Good,' the man says. 'White is best when there's snow. Nobody can see you. Now, are you ready? Let's go.'

They leave the house and walk quickly out of the village. After a time they stop and the man says, very quietly:

'OK. Do you see those trees? Turn right there and go fifty metres. When you come to the road, go across it quickly and run down the hill through the trees. Then you come to the river. Turn left and go 500 metres. The trees finish there and you can walk through the river easily. Across two more fields, and you're in Austria. Our friends are waiting for you in the second field. Go now. Goodbye

She does not see the black car under the trees.

– and good luck!'

The woman begins to run. The baby on her back is sleeping, but now he opens his eyes and begins to cry. The woman is afraid and runs more slowly, but the baby's crying is loud in the night. At the trees the woman turns right and soon she is at the road. She does not see the black car under the trees, but the men in the car see her.

Suddenly there is a noise in the night – the noise of guns. Then it is quiet again.

The woman's body lies in the snow on the road. Now the only sound is the crying of the baby.

2

England 1995

'Hey, Jan, look at this!' Carol said. She had a letter in her hand and took it across to her husband at the breakfast table. 'It's from the Oxford Orchestra,' she said. 'They're giving concerts in the Czech Republic this Christmas. They're doing three concerts in Prague and they're asking me to go because they need a harpist. Shall we go to Prague for Christmas? I can play with the orchestra, and you can come with us.'

'When are the concerts?' asked Jan. 'I always have a lot of work in the weeks before Christmas. I must finish writing my new book then.'

Jan taught Czech at Oxford University and wrote books about languages. He was born in Czechoslovakia, but came to England with his father when he was very young. He met Carol when she was one of his students at university.

'The first concert is on December 20th,' Carol answered. 'Are you free then?'

'No, I'm sorry, Carol,' Jan said, 'but I can't come before December 24th.'

'Well, it doesn't matter. You can come for the second concert. It's on December 25th.'

'But what about my father?' said Jan. 'We can't go away and leave him at Christmas time. He loves a family Christmas with us – you know that.'

Jan's father came slowly into the room.

Josef Vlach was sixty-eight years old, and his eyes were bad. He couldn't see very well, so he lived with Carol and Jan.

'Josef can come with us,' Carol said. 'He often talks about Prague at Christmas. He says it's the most beautiful time of the year there because of all the snow on the old buildings.'

'I know,' said Jan. 'But he only talks about Prague. He never wants to go there. Every time we ask him to come with us, he says no. I don't know why, but I think it's because of my mother. When he thinks about Prague, he remembers her. You know, sometimes he cries when he looks at his photo of her – after all these years!'

Just then the door opened and Jan's father came slowly into the room.

'Good morning,' he said, and sat down at the table. 'Is there any coffee?'

'It's cold now,' said Carol. 'Shall I make you some more?'

'Thank you, my dear,' he answered. 'You're very good to me.'

Carol went out for some coffee. Jan looked at his father carefully. 'I must ask him now,' he thought, 'while Carol is out of the room.'

'You're very quiet, Jan,' said the old man. 'Is something wrong?'

'No, no,' said Jan quickly. 'Nothing's wrong. It's just . . .

7

I want to ask you a question, but I . . . I . . . it's difficult.'

Jan stopped. His father smiled.

'Difficult? Why is it difficult? Are you afraid of an old man?'

'Of course not,' said Jan. 'But I *am* afraid of your answer. You see, Carol wants to go very much. She loves playing her harp, but it's Christmas time and—'

'Stop!' said Josef. 'What are you talking about? Where does Carol want to go at Christmas?'

'To Prague,' said Jan. 'And I would like to go with her. We want you to come too.'

'Ah!' said the old man. 'To Prague. I understand now.'

The room was suddenly very quiet. Jan drank his cold coffee and waited.

The old man took something out of his pocket. It was a photograph of his dead wife, Jan's mother. He spoke very quietly – not to Jan, but to the photograph in his hand.

'Perhaps now . . . before I die . . . just once I can go back again . . .'

Carol came back with some hot coffee. She looked at Josef, then at Jan.

'Shhh . . . He's thinking about Prague,' Jan said quietly.

Carol put the coffee on the table and sat down. The hands on the clock slowly moved through two long minutes. Then the old man put the photograph back in his pocket.

'All right,' he said. 'Let's all go to Prague for Christmas. It's beautiful there when it snows. I remember it so well . . . so very well.'

'Let's all go to Prague for Christmas.'

3

The accident

The first rehearsal began at nine o'clock and finished at two o'clock.

'What a long morning!' everyone said.

'I'm sorry,' said the conductor, 'but we have very little time. The first concert is tomorrow night and a lot of important people are coming, so we must play well. Now please go and eat. This afternoon is free, so you can go

We must play well.

'I must find something this afternoon.'

and look at this beautiful city. Tomorrow morning we begin again at nine o'clock. Please don't be late!'

Carol left the rehearsal room with Alan, one of the first violinists.

'What are you going to do this afternoon, Carol?' Alan asked.

'I'm going to get a quick sandwich, and then I'm going shopping,' Carol said. 'My husband Jan and his father are arriving on Sunday. Monday is Christmas Day, and I haven't got any presents for them. I must find something this afternoon – our only free afternoon.'

'See you tomorrow, then,' said Alan. 'And good luck with the shopping!'

11

'Thanks,' Carol said. 'There are some wonderful shops in the Stare Mesto, the old town, so I'm going down there.'

Carol went into a lot of shops that afternoon. In the end she got a book for Jan and a picture for his father. When she left the old town, it was nearly dark. It was very cold, so she walked quickly through the streets back to her hotel. There were Christmas trees in all the shop windows, and the city looked beautiful. There was a lot of noise too – people, cars, taxis, buses. 'Everybody's doing their Christmas shopping,' Carol thought.

'Jan! Jan! It's me, Carol!'

12

Suddenly she saw a man across the street. It was Jan! Why was he in Prague so soon?

'Jan!' she shouted across the street. But Jan didn't hear her. He walked on. Carol shouted again, very loudly.

'Jan! Jan! It's me, Carol!'

A lot of people stopped this time. They all looked at her. The man stopped too. He turned and looked at Carol for a minute, but he didn't smile and he didn't speak. It was a very long minute for Carol. Her husband's eyes were cold, and Carol began to feel afraid.

There was a sudden noise and somebody shouted.

Then he moved and began to walk away from Carol down a little street. Carol did not understand it, but she knew one thing – she did not want to lose him.

'Perhaps he didn't see me very well. It's so dark now . . . He's going . . . Where is he going? Jan, come back . . . Are you ill?'

She ran across the street.

There was a sudden noise and somebody shouted. Two seconds later Carol lay in the snow.

'She ran right in front of me,' the bus driver said later. 'I couldn't stop – there was no time.'

Carol's face was white and her eyes were closed. Soon an ambulance came and took her body away.

Was she alive or dead?

* * *

At nine o'clock the next morning the conductor was ready to begin the rehearsal. He opened his music and the orchestra started to play. Suddenly his hands stopped moving and the music stopped at once.

'Harpist!' the conductor shouted angrily. 'What's the matter with you? Are you sleeping? You begin to play here.'

'Excuse me, Mr Rinaldi,' said someone at the back of the room. 'The harpist is not here.'

Everyone turned and looked at the harp at the back of the orchestra. It was true. There was nobody in the harpist's chair.

'Well, where is she?' asked the conductor. There was no answer. 'We can't wait for her,' he said. 'We must have this rehearsal without her. Where is Alan? He can speak some Czech.'

Alan stood up.

'Can you go to the hotel and look for her there?' the conductor asked. 'Then come back here at once – with or without her.'

'Can you go to the hotel and look for her there?'

Alan left. Half an hour later he was back.

'She's not at the hotel,' he said. 'I spoke to two or three people in the hotel, and they say that Carol wasn't there at breakfast this morning. And they think that she didn't sleep in her room last night.'

'I don't like this,' said the conductor. 'Carol is never late for rehearsals, and she knows that these concerts are important for us. I think we must tell the police.'

'Shall I do it now?' Alan asked.

'Yes,' said the conductor. 'Please go now.'

4

Nobody understands Carol

Carol slowly opened her eyes. Her head hurt. She closed her eyes again.

A man said something. What was it?

'Carol,' she heard. 'Carol, can you hear me?'

'I can hear you,' Carol said. 'But I don't want to open my eyes. My head hurts. Who are you?'

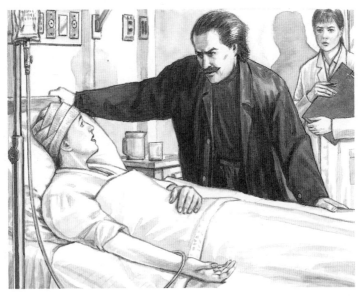

'Who are you?'

'It's me, Giorgio Rinaldi, the conductor of the orchestra.'

'Mr Rinaldi?' Carol opened her eyes again. Her head didn't hurt so much this time.

'What are you doing in my bedroom?' she asked angrily. 'What's happening?'

'This isn't your bedroom,' said Mr Rinaldi. 'It's a hospital in Prague. You had an accident yesterday. Can you remember anything about it?'

Suddenly Carol remembered everything. The old town . . . the Christmas trees in the shop windows . . . Christmas presents . . . Jan . . . *Jan!*

She sat up.

'Jan! Where's Jan?' she asked Mr Rinaldi.

'Please, Mrs Vlach,' said a woman quietly. 'Don't get excited. Lie down again.'

Carol turned her head. It hurt again. Near the door of the room she saw a woman in a white coat – a doctor.

'But I must see Jan,' Carol said. 'Where is he? I must find him . . . I can't . . . Oh, dear.' She put her hand to her head.

'Who's Jan?' the doctor asked Mr Rinaldi quietly.

'Her husband,' he answered. He took Carol's hand. 'Listen, your husband is coming. We told him about the accident. He's on a plane from London now.'

'On a plane? Why? He's here in Prague. I saw him in the street, near the old town. I called out to him, and he saw me, but he didn't stop . . . He just walked away from me. Please find him . . . please . . . I must talk to him . . . I must . . .'

The doctor moved nearer to the bed.

'Jan is coming soon, Mrs Vlach,' she said. 'Please don't get excited. It's not good for you. Now, lie down again and close your eyes. You must sleep, and I know you're feeling very tired.'

Carol lay down and closed her eyes. The doctor was right. She was tired. But why didn't they listen? Why didn't they understand? Jan was in Prague, and she must find him . . . talk to him . . .

The doctor looked at Mr Rinaldi and spoke very quietly. 'Let's leave her now, please. She needs to sleep. You can come back later.'

Mr Rinaldi and the doctor left the room. They closed the door quietly, and then looked at Carol through the window in the door.

'She's going to be all right,' said the doctor. 'She just needs to sleep for a time. There's nothing wrong with her.'

'Yes, there is!' said Mr Rinaldi. 'She thinks her husband is in Prague. But I spoke to him on the telephone three hours ago and he was in Oxford. I'm afraid she's ill – very ill.'

'Listen,' said the doctor. 'She had a bad hit on the head in the accident, but she didn't break anything and her head

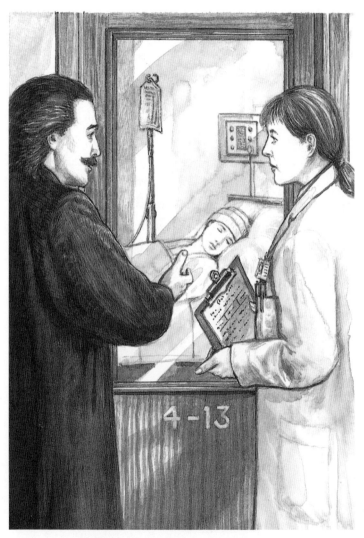

'She thinks her husband is in Prague.'

is all right. We looked at it very carefully. She's going to be OK after a good sleep.'

'But – all this talk about Jan her husband,' said Mr Rinaldi. 'What about that?'

'Yes, she's confused about that, it's true. But she remembers her name, she knows you, and she understands that she's in hospital. All this is very good. Now, what about you, Mr Rinaldi? It's a difficult time for you too, because of your concerts. I understand that. But please go away now. Eat something. Have a sleep. Then come back later this afternoon. You can't do anything now.'

'All right,' said Mr Rinaldi. But he was not happy.

'Poor Carol,' he thought. 'And my poor orchestra. How can I find another harpist before tonight's concert?'

5

Some visitors for Carol

Two hours later a tall man arrived at the hospital. He asked to see the woman in yesterday's street accident. He didn't know her name. The doctor came downstairs.

'Who are you?' she asked the man.

'My name is Pavel Brychta. I saw the accident and I called the ambulance. Is the woman all right? I just wanted to know that. I was afraid she was dead.'

The doctor smiled. 'Would you like to see her? She's much better now.'

'Yes, please,' answered Pavel.

'Then come with me.'

They went upstairs in the lift and walked along to Carol's room. At the door they stopped and looked in through the window.

'She's sleeping,' said the doctor.

'But she looks well,' said Pavel. 'Yesterday she looked so white! I was afraid for her.'

Just then Carol opened her eyes and saw a man through the window in her door.

She sat up. 'Jan!' she shouted. 'Jan!'

'Oh dear!' the doctor said. 'Not again! She hit her head

23

in the accident and she's confused about some things. She thinks that you are her husband from England.'

'Shall I go?' asked Pavel.

'Perhaps it's better – yes,' answered the doctor.

She went into Carol's room and closed the door. Pavel walked slowly back to the lift. Then the lift door opened and a man ran out, with some beautiful red flowers in his

He saw Pavel, and stopped suddenly.

24

arms. He looked at the numbers of the rooms and then went quickly into Carol's room. He didn't see Pavel. But an older man came slowly out of the lift next. He saw Pavel, and stopped suddenly. Pavel stopped too.

'I'm sorry,' said the old man. 'My eyes aren't very good . . . I thought . . . You see, you look—'

'Yes, I know,' said Pavel. 'I saw your friend.'

'He's not my friend – he's my son. Please, tell me, what is your name?'

'Pavel Brychta.'

The old man looked very afraid. His face went white, and his mouth opened and closed, but he said nothing.

Now Pavel was afraid.

'You don't look very well,' he said. 'Would you like to sit down? And shall I call a doctor? There's a doctor in this room here . . .'

'Please . . .' said the old man. 'My son is in that room. Please take me to him.'

Pavel took the old man's arm.

* * *

In Carol's room Jan put the red flowers on the bed and took his wife's hands.

'Oh, my love, are you all right?' he said. 'I can't understand it. Why did you run in front of a bus? How did it happen?'

Carol didn't answer his questions.

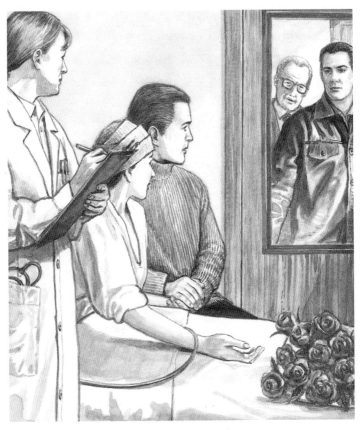

'Who–is–that?'

'Jan?' She looked up into his face. 'You *are* Jan? Tell me that you're Jan.'

'Of course I'm Jan! What are you talking about?'

The doctor came up to the bed. 'Wait a minute,' she

said. 'You told me that your name was Pavel Brychta. Are you Mrs Vlach's husband, or not?'

Just then Carol looked behind Jan. She saw Pavel with Jan's father through the window of her door. Her eyes got bigger and bigger.

'Who – is – that?' she said.

Jan and the doctor turned and saw Pavel.

'My God!' said Jan. 'I don't know!'

The doctor looked back at Jan's face. 'Two men, but only one face,' she said quietly.

Then Jan's father opened the door of Carol's room and the two men came in.

Jan stood up. He looked at his father. 'Who *is* this man?' he asked.

'His name is Pavel Brychta,' answered his father. 'Please bring me a chair and some water. I need to sit down before I can answer your question.'

Jan got a chair for his father and the doctor gave him some water. Then she left the room quietly.

6

Who is Pavel?

The old man drank some water and looked up.
'Pavel,' he said. 'I must ask you to look at this photo.'
He put his hand in his pocket and took out a photograph
of a young woman. 'Do you know this woman?'

'Yes,' said Pavel. 'That's a photo of my mother, Lenka.

'Do you know this woman?'

She died when I was very young. But my grandmother had many photos of her, and we often looked at them.'

'Did you live with your grandmother when you were young?'

'Yes, I did. But how do you know all this?'

'Because,' said Josef, 'Lenka was my wife.'

'Dad, what are you saying?' said Jan.

Josef looked at Jan. 'My boy, don't be angry with me. I didn't tell you many things about your mother. Perhaps I was wrong. But I wanted to forget . . . not to forget your mother, only to forget that terrible night in 1957. Jan, this man Pavel is your twin brother. You can see that it's true. Look at your faces.'

Pavel looked at Jan. 'So, I have a brother,' he said. 'My grandmother never told me that.'

Jan smiled. 'And my father – our father – never told *me* about a twin brother!' He turned to Josef. 'Dad, why didn't you tell me?'

'It's a long story,' said the old man. 'It begins many years ago when a young man went to Prague University. He was there for seven years, and in his last year he met a beautiful young woman.'

His eyes turned to the photo.

'She was so beautiful! Of course, the young man fell in love with her, and they got married in 1956. But things were difficult in Prague then. People were not happy and

29

they were not free. Lenka and I, and a lot of our friends, wanted to change things. But it was dangerous work. The Russians knew about us and they watched us all the time. Then you two boys were born on a wonderful day in June 1957.'

'But you went away,' Pavel said angrily. 'Your wife died, and you left the country. You went away to England and began a new life. You didn't write, you didn't telephone. You weren't interested in me – your son!'

Josef's face was very sad. 'Pavel,' he said. 'I thought you were dead. Look. I must show you something.' From

'You weren't interested in me – your son!'

behind the photo of his wife he took out a letter, and gave it to Pavel.

The letter was old and yellow. Pavel opened it and began to read. The letter was in Czech, and it was his grandmother's writing.

I write to tell you, Josef, that your wife is dead. On Christmas night the guards shot her on the road at the border. She carried Pavel – your baby son, and my grandson – on her back, and the guards shot him too. Your wife, and your son, are dead. Your 'friends' came and told me yesterday.

You have Jan, and a new life in England. And what do I have? Nothing. You took one grandson away from me, and now my daughter and little Pavel are dead – because of you. Don't write to me, and don't come back to Prague. I never want to see you or hear from you again.

Stanislava

Slowly, Pavel put the letter down. 'I understand now,' he said quietly. 'What a terrible letter! How could she do that to you . . . and to me?'

'Stanislava loved her daughter very much,' Josef said sadly. 'She loved you, too, and didn't want to lose you. I see that now. But she never liked me. And after that letter, how could I go back to Prague? You were dead, Lenka was dead . . .' He put his face in his hands.

The room was very quiet. Then Pavel put his hand on his father's arm. 'Stanislava is dead now,' he said. 'You and I can begin again . . .' He smiled. 'And learn to be father and son.'

Josef's face was wet with tears. He put his hand over Pavel's hand and smiled back at him, but he could not speak. Now there were tears in everybody's eyes.

After a minute or two Jan said, 'Dad, I know it's difficult for you. But can you tell us about that Christmas in 1957? How did it all happen? I'd like to know . . .'

'Yes,' said his father. 'You, and Pavel, must know.' He turned to Pavel. 'But what did Stanislava tell you?'

'Very little,' Pavel said. 'She never wanted to talk about it. She told me that my mother died in hospital. And you went away to England. That was all.'

'I can understand that,' said Josef. 'Poor Stanislava! She lost her daughter, because of me. And she never liked our work for freedom, you see. She didn't understand. She just wanted a quiet family life.'

'Christmas 1957 . . .' said Jan.

'Yes,' said Josef. 'In October and November of that year things got more and more dangerous for Lenka and me. Our friends told us: "Leave, before the Russians get you.

'Leave, before the Russians get you.'

Get away to Austria, and then to England." We didn't want to leave Czechoslovakia, of course; it was our home. But we couldn't stay. Our friends helped us, and Jan and I got across the border on the day before Christmas, December the 24th. It was night. There was no moon, and we got to Austria all right through the fields and the snow. But the next night . . .'

'December the 25th,' said Pavel. 'My grandmother told me the day. My mother died in a hospital bed in Prague, she said.'

'Lenka died in the snow, on the road at the border,' Josef said. 'She was so near Austria . . . so near us . . . with you, Pavel, on her back . . .'

The old man's voice stopped, and again, he put his head in his hands.

7

The music must come first

For some minutes nobody in the room said anything. They looked at the old man in his chair, and they all thought about a snowy night in 1957.

Then Pavel turned to Jan.

'Let's forget 1957 for now,' he said quietly. 'For me, this is a wonderful day. I have no family in Prague. My grandmother died many years ago. But now I have a

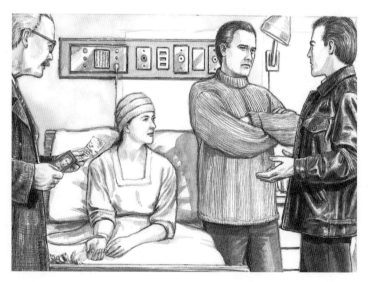

'Let's forget 1957 for now.'

brother, a father . . .' He looked at Carol in her bed, and smiled. 'And a sister.'

'Why did you come to the hospital to see me?' Carol asked.

'You had an accident because of me,' Pavel said. 'I knew that. You called to me, and shouted, and then ran to me across the street, right in front of a bus. I didn't understand why, but I wanted to know that you were all right.'

Jan looked at Carol too. 'And *are* you all right, my love? I'm sorry, I forgot about you . . .'

'I'm feeling very well,' Carol said happily. 'Now I understand everything, so I feel much better. My husband is my husband again – and we have a new brother. Oh, but there is one thing . . .' She looked at her new brother. 'Why is your name Pavel Brychta, and not Pavel Vlach?'

The old man moved in his chair. 'Her name was Lenka Brychta,' he said quietly, 'before she married me.'

'Yes,' Pavel said. He looked at Carol. 'You see, my father didn't want me, I thought. So I didn't want my father's name, and when I was older, I changed it and took my mother's name.' He turned to his father. 'I was an angry young man then, but now . . .'

'No,' said Josef. 'Don't change it. It's a very good name. And you are Lenka's son.'

Suddenly the door opened, and Mr Rinaldi came in.

'Carol,' he said, 'the doctor says that you are better. Is

Suddenly the door opened, and Mr Rinaldi came in.

it true? You look wonderful. Can you play in the concert tonight? You see, I can't find another harpist, and without a harp the music—'

He saw everyone for the first time, and stopped.

'Oh, I'm sorry,' he said quickly. 'I see you have friends here. But, you see, it's important. It's an important concert for my orchestra and—' He stopped again. 'Why are you all laughing at me?'

Jan stopped laughing first.

'Mr Rinaldi,' he said, 'you are the right man for Prague, the city of music. The music must come first!'

'Carol . . .' Mr Rinaldi began.

Carol turned to Jan. 'I feel very well now and I'd like to play tonight. But I want all my family to come to the concert – my husband, my new brother, and their father. Can you all come? Please say yes!'

Jan looked at his father.

'Are you all right, dad? Or are you feeling tired now? Shall we all go to Mr Rinaldi's concert?'

'Free tickets, of course, for all Carol's family,' said Mr Rinaldi quickly.

'Christmas music in Prague again,' Josef said slowly. 'And with my two sons. Wonderful, wonderful . . .' He smiled happily at Jan and Pavel.

'How can we say no?' he asked.

GLOSSARY

border   the line between two countries

bus   a kind of big 'car' which many people can travel in

city   a big town

concert   a time when an orchestra plays music to many people

conductor   a conductor stands in front of an orchestra and
shows them when to play the music quickly, slowly, quietly,
etc.

confused *(adj)*   when you cannot understand something, you
feel confused

dangerous   something dangerous can hurt or kill you

difficult   not easy

fall in love with   to begin to love somebody

field   a piece of ground where animals eat grass, or people grow
food

freedom   being free

get married   to take someone as a husband or wife

guard *(n)*   someone who watches a border, or buildings, etc. to
stop people coming in or going out

gun   a thing that shoots out bullets to kill people

harp   a musical instrument with many strings, played with the
fingers

harpist   a person who plays the harp

hurt   to feel pain

lie (past tense **lay**)   to put your body flat on something, e.g. a
bed, the ground

lift *(n)*   a kind of large 'box' that takes people up and down in a
high building

loud   not quiet; with a lot of noise

moon   the big round thing that shines in the sky at night
music   when you sing or play an instrument, you make music
orchestra   a group of people who play musical instruments together
police   people who look for bad people and send them to prison, and who help when dangerous things like accidents happen
poor   when you say 'poor', you are feeling sorry for somebody
present   something which you give to somebody at Christmas, on birthdays, etc.
rehearsal   when you practise music, etc. before you do it in front of other people
sad   not happy
shoot (past tense **shot**)   to send a bullet from a gun and kill or hurt somebody
shout *(v)*   to speak or call out very loudly
snow   rain which is very cold and white; it comes down slowly and lies on the ground
tears   water which comes from the eyes
terrible   very, very bad
turn   to move your body round
twin   one of two children who are born of the same mother at the same time
university   a place where people go to study after they leave school
violin   a small musical instrument with four strings
violinist   a person who plays the violin
wet   not dry; full of water

Christmas in Prague

ACTIVITIES

Before Reading

1 The title of the story is *Christmas in Prague*. Find the answers to these questions.

    1 Where is Prague?

    2 Was life in Prague in 1957 very different from life there in 1995? How?

2 What do people do at Christmas in Britain and many other countries? Make three sentences. Use some of the words from this list.

dinner, family, music, presents, children, holiday

3 Read the back cover of the book. How much do you know now about the story? Tick one box for each sentence.

	YES	NO
1 Carol and Jan are married.	☐	☐
2 Carol's father is called Josef.	☐	☐
3 Josef is English.	☐	☐
4 Josef lived in Prague a long time ago.	☐	☐
5 Josef is afraid to go back to Prague.	☐	☐

4 Read the story introduction on the first page of the book. Are these sentences true (T) or false (F)? Change the false sentences into true ones.

1 Jan was born in London.
2 Jan's mother lives in Oxford with her son.
3 Josef often talks about his wife.
4 Josef has a photograph of Jan's mother in his pocket.
5 Carol plays the guitar.
6 Carol wants to go to Prague for Christmas.

5 What are the family secrets in the story? Can you guess? Tick one box for each sentence.

	YES	NO
1 Someone in the family is dead.	☐	☐
2 Someone in the family is alive.	☐	☐
3 Someone in the family is in prison.	☐	☐
4 Someone in the family has got a lot of money.	☐	☐
5 You guess! _____		

While Reading

Read Chapter 1. Underline the mistakes in this paragraph and then correct them.

It is midday. This is Czechoslovakia and the year is 1967. Across the fields is the German border. In a house, a man and a woman are talking. The woman holds a baby girl in her arms. She puts on a black coat and a black hat. They leave the house and walk slowly out of the village. The man says goodbye and the woman begins to run. The baby opens his eyes and is very quiet. At the trees, the woman turns left and soon she is at the river. She sees a black car but the men in the car do not see her.

Read Chapters 2 and 3, then answer these questions.

Who

1 . . . wanted to go to Prague to play in some concerts?
2 . . . was writing a new book?
3 . . . talked about Prague but never wanted to go there?
4 . . . went shopping in Prague?
5 . . . looked at Carol in the street, but didn't smile?
6 . . . couldn't stop because there was no time?
7 . . . was angry because Carol was not at the rehearsal?

Before you read Chapter 4, can you guess what happens?
Tick one box for each sentence.

	YES	NO
1 Carol is dead.	☐	☐
2 Carol is in hospital, but she can't remember anything.	☐	☐
3 Carol is in hospital and she is going to be OK.	☐	☐

Read Chapters 4 and 5. Choose the best question-word for
these questions, and then answer them.

Why / What / How

1 . . . did Carol feel when she woke up in hospital?
2 . . . did Mr Rinaldi think that Carol was very ill?
3 . . . was it a difficult time for Mr Rinaldi?
4 . . . did Carol shout 'Jan' when she saw Pavel through
the window in her door?
5 . . . did Jan bring for Carol?
6 . . . did the doctor say about Jan and Pavel?

Read Chapters 6 and 7. Put these sentences in the correct
order, and complete them. (Use as many words as you like.)

1 Carol played in the concert and her family _____.
2 Pavel changed his name because _____.
3 Pavel found that he had a father, a brother _____.
4 Stanislava said Pavel was dead because _____.
5 Stanislava told Pavel that his mother died _____.

After Reading

1 Fill in the names in this family tree, and then write ten sentences about the people. Use these words.

father, mother, son, grandmother, brother, wife, husband
Example: *Josef is Jan's father.*

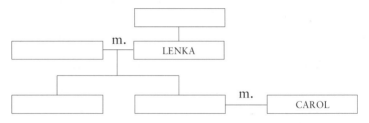

2 What happened in 1956 and 1957? Match these halves of sentences and join them with these words.

and / because / but / so

1 Josef and Lenka got married
2 Josef and Lenka wanted to change things in Czechoslovakia
3 Josef and Lenka couldn't stay in Czechoslovakia
4 Josef carried Jan across the border on 24th December
5 Lenka tried to cross the border with Pavel on 25th December
6 Stanislava didn't want to lose Pavel

7 _____ she told Josef that his wife and son were dead.

8 _____ after that they went to England.

9 _____ had two sons, Jan and Pavel.

10 _____ it was dangerous.

11 _____ people were not free or happy.

12 _____ the guards shot her.

3 Mr Rinaldi telephoned Jan to tell him about Carol's accident. Write out the conversation in the correct order and put in the speakers' names. Rinaldi speaks first (3).

1 _____ 'An accident? What happened?'

2 _____ 'Carol! It's Carol, isn't it? Tell me, quickly!'

3 _____ 'Hello? Mr Vlach? This is Mr Rinaldi, from the orchestra.'

4 _____ 'Yes, I'm afraid I have some bad news for you.'

5 _____ 'In hospital? But why? Is she ill?'

6 _____ 'Oh no! I must come at once. I'm going to catch the next plane to Prague. Please tell her that I'm coming.'

7 _____ 'She had a little accident in the street yesterday.'

8 _____ 'Yes, it's Carol. She's in hospital, but she's going to be all right, Mr Vlach, I promise you.'

9 _____ 'She ran in front of a bus and the bus hit her.'

10 _____ 'Yes. What is it? Is something wrong?'

4 Here is a new illustration for the story. Find the best place
in the story to put the picture, and answer these questions.

The picture goes on page _____.

1 Who is the woman in the bed and why is she in hospital?

2 Why is she shouting?

3 Why is the man there?

Now write a caption for the illustration.

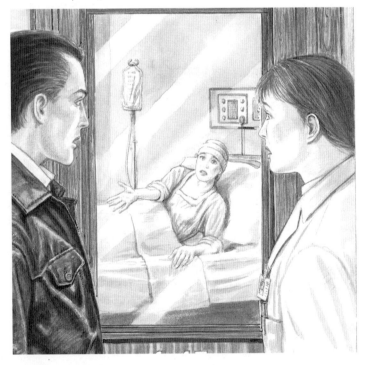

Caption: _____

5 **Imagine that Stanislava wrote a different letter and told Josef the true story. Use these words to complete her letter. (Use each word once.)**

alive, baby, back, border, but, dangerous, daughter, dead, didn't, guards, have, her, him, new, stay, tell, with, write

I write to _____ you, Josef, that your wife is _____. On Christmas night the _____ shot her on the road at the _____. She carried Pavel – your _____ son, and my grandson – on _____ back, but the guards _____ shoot him. Your wife is dead _____ your son is _____. Your 'friends' brought _____ to me yesterday.

You have Jan and a _____ life in England. And I _____ baby Pavel. But my _____ is dead. I want Pavel to _____ here with me. Don't _____ to me, and don't come _____ to Prague. It is _____. Pavel is all right _____ me.
Stanislava

6 **Do you agree (A) or disagree (D) with these sentences? Explain why.**

1 Stanislava was a bad person because she told Josef a lie.
2 Stanislava was very unhappy, not bad.
3 Josef and Lenka were wrong to do dangerous things when they had two babies.
4 Josef and Lenka were right to work for freedom; that was more important than their children.

ABOUT THE AUTHOR

Joyce Hannam is an experienced teacher and lecturer. She has taught English in several European countries, including Greece, Spain, Turkey, and the Czech Republic. She now lives in York, in the north of England, and works mostly with Japanese university students and business people from Germany, Italy, France and Spain. Her stories for the Oxford Bookworms Library also include *The Death of Karen Silkwood* (at Stage 2), in the True Stories series.

Joyce Hannam is married to a musician and has one young daughter. All three of them enjoy singing at all times and in all places. Her story *Christmas in Prague* was inspired by a visit to that city.

ABOUT BOOKWORMS

OXFORD BOOKWORMS LIBRARY
Classics • True Stories • Fantasy & Horror • Human Interest
Crime & Mystery • Thriller & Adventure

The OXFORD BOOKWORMS LIBRARY offers a wide range of original and adapted stories, both classic and modern, which take learners from elementary to advanced level through six carefully graded language stages:

Stage 1 (400 headwords)	**Stage 4** (1400 headwords)
Stage 2 (700 headwords)	**Stage 5** (1800 headwords)
Stage 3 (1000 headwords)	**Stage 6** (2500 headwords)

More than fifty titles are also available on cassette, and there are many titles at Stages 1 to 4 which are specially recommended for younger learners. In addition to the introductions and activities in each Bookworm, resource material includes photocopiable test worksheets and Teacher's Handbooks, which contain advice on running a class library and using cassettes, and the answers for the activities in the books.

———————————

Several other series are linked to the OXFORD BOOKWORMS LIBRARY. They range from highly illustrated readers for young learners, to playscripts, non-fiction readers, and unsimplified texts for advanced learners.

Oxford Bookworms Starters	*Oxford Bookworms Factfiles*
Oxford Bookworms Playscripts	*Oxford Bookworms Collection*

Details of these series and a full list of all titles in the OXFORD BOOKWORMS LIBRARY can be found in the *Oxford English* catalogues. A selection of titles from the OXFORD BOOKWORMS LIBRARY can be found on the next pages.

The Lottery Winner
ROSEMARY BORDER

Everybody wants to win the lottery. A million pounds, perhaps five million, even ten million. How wonderful! Emma Carter buys a ticket for the lottery every week, and puts the ticket carefully in her bag. She is seventy-three years old and does not have much money. She would like to visit her son in Australia, but aeroplane tickets are very expensive.

Jason Williams buys lottery tickets every week too. But he is not a very nice young man. He steals things. He hits old ladies in the street, snatches their bags and runs away . . .

Remember Miranda
ROWENA AKINYEMI

Cathy Wilson is driving to Norfolk, to begin her new job with the Harvey family. She is going to look after the two young children, Tim and Susan. Cathy meets the children's father, and their grandmother, and their aunt. She meets Nick, the farmer who lives across the fields. But she doesn't meet Miranda, the children's mother, because Miranda is dead.

She died two years ago, and Cathy cannot learn anything about her. Everybody remembers Miranda, but nobody wants to talk about her . . .

BOOKWORMS • HUMAN INTEREST • STAGE 1
One-Way Ticket

JENNIFER BASSETT

Tom Walsh had a lot to learn about life. He liked travelling, and he was in no hurry. He liked meeting people, anyone and everyone. He liked the two American girls on the train. They were nice and very friendly. They knew a lot of places. Tom thought they were fun. Tom certainly had a lot to learn about life.

This is a collection of short stories about adventures on trains. Strange, wonderful, and frightening things can happen on trains – and all of them happen here.

BOOKWORMS • CRIME & MYSTERY • STAGE 1
Love or Money?

ROWENA AKINYEMI

It is Molly Clarkson's fiftieth birthday. She is having a party. She is rich, but she is having a small party – only four people. Four people, however, who all need the same thing: they need her money. She will not give them the money, so they are waiting for her to die. And there are other people who are also waiting for her to die.

But one person can't wait. And so, on her fiftieth birthday, Molly Clarkson is going to die.

White Death

TIM VICARY

Sarah Harland is nineteen, and she is in prison. At the airport, they find heroin in her bag. So, now she is waiting to go to court. If the court decides that it was her heroin, then she must die.

She says she did not do it. But if she did not, who did? Only two people can help Sarah: her mother, and an old boyfriend who does not love her now. Can they work together? Can they find the real criminal before it is too late?

The Piano

ROSEMARY BORDER

One day, a farmer tells a farm boy to take everything out of an old building and throw it away. 'It's all rubbish,' he says.

In the middle of all the rubbish, the boy finds a beautiful old piano. He has never played before, but now, when his fingers touch the piano, he begins to play. He closes his eyes and the music comes to him – and the music moves his fingers.

When he opens his eyes again, he knows that his life is changed for ever . . .